Red Line—Carbon Dioxide
How humans saved
all life on Earth
by burning fossil fuels

More books by Rod Martin, Jr.

Climate Basics: Nothing to Fear—#1 Bestseller on Amazon, in Weather and Science & Math short reads. Debunks the key points of warming alarmism.

Deserts & Droughts: How does land ever get water?—Book 2 in the *Climate Basics series*.

Thermophobia: Shining a Light on Global Warming—Taking the terror out of Global Warming. Giving the proper perspective on this, the most prosperous period in human history.

Red Line —Carbon Dioxide

How humans saved all life on Earth by burning fossil fuels

Rod Martin, Jr.

Tharsis Highlands Publishing
Cebu, Philippines

Published by Tharsis Highlands Publishing
Cebu, Philippines
https://tharsishighlands.wordpress.com/books/

Amazon Print Edition
May 2019
ISBN: 9781070247434

EBook Editions
Amazon Kindle—2016, 2018
Smashwords—2016, 2018

Cover photo: Plants at Modhupur forest by Ferdous (CC BY-SA 4.0), and dry plants by Francisco Antunes (CC BY 2.0).
Cover design: Rod Martin, Jr.

Typography fonts
Headings: Rockwell Extra Bold
Running Heads: Rockwell
Text: Palatino Linotype

"Frugality drives innovation, just like other constraints do. One of the only ways to get out of a tight box is to invent your way out."
—Jeff Bezos

Table of Contents

Introduction: The Real Threats of Climate Change

One of the most positive effects of the modern debate on "climate change" is that more and more people have started to care about the environment. Sadly, the acrimonious state of the debate has eroded some of that care. Too often the corporate mainstream media uses words like "denier," or "climate denier" and at times has seemed to lose its objectivity, crying for those who disagree to be jailed or worse. Anyone who wants to lock up people for their viewpoints is no friend of humanity. If minds are to be changed, cordial debate is the only way. Anything else tends to look like criminal intent and an urge to hide something.

When NASA posted a page on their website dedicated to "scientific consensus," they removed themselves as a scientific agency and turned themselves into a political one. The term itself is an *oxymoron*—a self-contradictory phrase. Science is never done by consensus (popularity or voting). That my late father ever worked indirectly for this agency has become a mark of ignominy.

In a very real sense, the pseudo-science and anti-science surrounding this topic have taken on the trappings of a new Dark Ages. Even President Obama has stooped pretty low in discussing the climate debate. For instance, he criticized any sharp analysis leveled against the "consensus." He compared it with membership in the "flat Earth society" (LoGiurato). As a marketing ploy, this might work with the weak minded. But it shows a level of underhandedness and flabby ethics on the part of this president who also holds several other dark demerits—a Nobel Peace prize while becoming the most war mongering president in American history (continuing three wars while starting at least one other, and threatening more), and a kill list (Becker; Swann), including his own citizens, which betrays his oath of office to uphold the Constitution of the United States. These are social and political threats. They undermine the very fabric of civilization.

These criticisms I've made of the people and organizations who have stirred the pot of discontent a little too vigorously are *ad hominem* logical fallacies, if we are debating the merits of the "climate change" claims. They are "to the man," so to speak, instead of to the topic at hand. So, let's switch gears here. Let's look at the facts related to this topic and not the personalities involved.

Demonizing global warming in an ongoing Ice Age is perhaps a far more immediate threat. This remains especially critical, because our current interglacial—the Holocene—is already as much as 6,000 years older than the average interglacial of the current Ice Age (Broecker). That most people don't realize that we live in an Ice Age only exacerbates the problem.

If our actions, combined with natural forces, trigger the catastrophic end of the Holocene, then we could see an abrupt end to civilization as we know it. Incidents like the Great Ice

Storm of 1998 amplify the fragile nature of our technological infrastructure (CBC). Our citizens have become reliant on the technology and have lost the self-reliance that could save them should something like permanent glaciation happen. An abrupt end to the Holocene could give Earth 90,000 years without summers, rain, crops, food, and civilization. That may seem harsh, but it's entirely realistic, given our inability to respond to minor natural disasters, like hurricane Katrina. A full-blown, global glacial period is several orders of magnitude more dangerous than a local, category 5 hurricane.

This book is dedicated to hard facts that reveal some aspects of the climate debate that are too rarely discussed in scientific circles, and rarely, if ever seen in the media.

Polar Bear Fantasies

Two of nature's key benefits have been dragged through the popular press and slandered beyond all recognition. Someone has mounted a clever marketing campaign to sell danger as a benefit, and benefit as a danger. Pictures flash on our television screens of "helpless" polar bears struggling to get on top of thin ice, and people are in tears (BBC). Little do they know that such emotional ploys are empty of meaning. They are appeals to emotion, also logical fallacies.

Polar bears are strong, powerful swimmers, so this notion that they can't handle themselves in the open ocean is incorrect. Their numbers are increasing, because warmth means more food. Some nature lovers seem to imply that bears can't get food any other way than through holes in the ice or at the edge of the ice. That's where they catch the lipid-rich ice seals. But some polar bears have already started living off of land-based food sources—"may be eating terrestrial foods including berries, birds and eggs" (Watts, 2015:0403). So far, such incursions into land-based dining appear to be rare, but scientists suspect that polar bears originally evolved from brown bears. No doubt, the urge to survive will help them adapt to the changes.

We could let Earth slip into the next glacial period and give polar bears more of the ice that helps them capture seals, or we could be compassionate for *all* life *and* civilization and give polar bears food during the transition to a warmer planet. That is, if we were to figure out how to end the current Ice Age and melt all the ice. Change is inevitable. Some change is far worse than global warming.

Some climate skeptics had once thought that polar bears had several hundred or even a few thousand years without sea ice during the Eemian interglacial. I was one of them. That geological period was as much as +5°C warmer than today's global average temperature. According to a study published in 2012, even though the Eemian was far warmer, the Arctic appears to have been cooler in at least one location. Deep sea sediment cores off the coast of Ireland contain proxies indicating far warmer temperatures characteristic of the Eemian. But researchers found something strange in sediment cores taken east of Jan Mayen Island in the Arctic Sea, northeast of Iceland. They found indications that the area was colder than expected. The scientists suspect that the Gulf Stream was somehow far weaker back then (Phys.org). It's also possible that the Gulf Stream was blocked back then so that it could not reach the Arctic Ocean north of Europe (Martin, 2010).

Ironically, Greenland, farther west, lost a lot of ice during the Eemian. So, the Jan Mayen results are not con-clusive for the Arctic as a whole. Much of the coastal hinterlands were ice free for thousands of years. Also, sea level was far higher than today. One core in the Arctic does not mean that all of the Arctic region was cold. More research is needed. It's still possible that most, if not all polar bears were without sea ice, and survived quite well.

Ice Fetish?

Wishing for global cooling in an Ice Age is like wishing for empty plates at a banquet when you're starving. Yes, it's that simple. Ice is deadly. A small minority of species have adapted to an ice environment. We could cave in and let ice destroy many other species and civilization, or we could get smart and help polar bears and coastal citizens over the transition to a warmer, healthier Earth.

While any change in climate will cause problems, most of the problems from warming remain extremely minor. Life will adapt; it always has. And humans could help polar bears, if we were compassionate. The only major problem with global warming is from rising sea levels. This one problem could cost a few trillion dollars in rebuilding, moving and erecting dikes where possible. But that is tiny compared to the loss of life and property if the Holocene ends and those two little white things at the poles persist to become huge.

I, for one, place more value on life than coastal real estate. With global warming, I will also have to move. But it's a small price to pay for saving civilization, 7 billion lives and likely trillions of land animals.

Imagine your senior years, looking back at your life and how things turned out. Here are two possibilities:

1)   Sitting on your sun deck, wrapped in a jacket to protect you against the new cold, you look out over the receding ocean, happy that your coastal estate isn't flooded, but sad that most everyone on the planet is now dead, and that civilization's infrastructure has become decimated by the growing glaciation and desiccation. Food is scarce because of the lack of rain. Your grandchildren

have a bleak future. They will have to keep the flame of civilization alive for 90,000 years or so, until the next interglacial makes the rebirth of civilization possible.

2)   Living in your new home, away from the now flooded coast, you enjoy new opportunities for farming on what once was frozen land. Civilization continues to thrive, giving up its childish ways of war and collectivist haranguing. Volunteers help feed the polar bears while they adapt to the new, warmer climate. Strong storms are disappearing. Deserts are shrinking and the tropics are booming in prosperity now that hurricanes and typhoons are largely a thing of the past. Your grand-children have a bright future filled with opportunities.

Admittedly, these are simplistic views of two possible future extremes. But they help illustrate the critical differences we face.

This book is all about the wacky world of "climate change," focusing on the wrongly slandered and vital gas of life—carbon dioxide. CO_2 has been accused of making the Earth become dangerously warm. Both the claim and the implication are lies. This book will show that carbon dioxide does not drive the planet's temperature (though it does contribute a minor amount to warming). More importantly, it will be shown that global warming is good, thus CO_2 is not guilty of any crime.

Climate is a complex, non-linear system, but it obeys rather simple laws that are easy to understand. Things get messy when we try to nail down the exact degree or the exact state at some future date or specific location. But the basics are straightforward and uncomplicated.

Chapter 1 — 15,000 BC, Dodging the CO_2 Extinction Bullet

Approximately 15,000 BC, carbon dioxide levels became dangerously low. Though not every species of plant reacts the same way to such shortages, a common rule of thumb puts a minimum limit on CO_2 at 150 ppm (parts per million by volume) (Lovelock).

As a rough rule of thumb, 150 ppm would result in the death of many species and a severe degradation to many other species. Whenever Earth's atmosphere reaches this level, or lower, it will have passed the "Red Line" of death, and entered the zone of mass extinction. Combine the scarcity of CO_2 with the lack of warmth and rain during a glacial period, and life would become stressed to the maximum.

If all plants die from a lack of CO_2, then all animal life will soon follow. The reason for this is simple, but it's worth making this point explicitly clear—if plants die, animals will no longer have food. Most all life on Earth will end up dying.

Perhaps a few anaerobic species will continue at the bottom of the ocean.

About 15,000 BC, CO_2 levels reached 180 ppm—that's only 30 ppm above our "Red Line" of death. During the last several glacial periods of the current Ice Age, CO_2 levels have dipped below 200 ppm. As more and more carbon dioxide is sunk into sedimentation, the glacial period levels keep getting lower and lower, aiming toward zero. The CO_2 level that is ultimately reached in each glacial period depends on a number of factors.

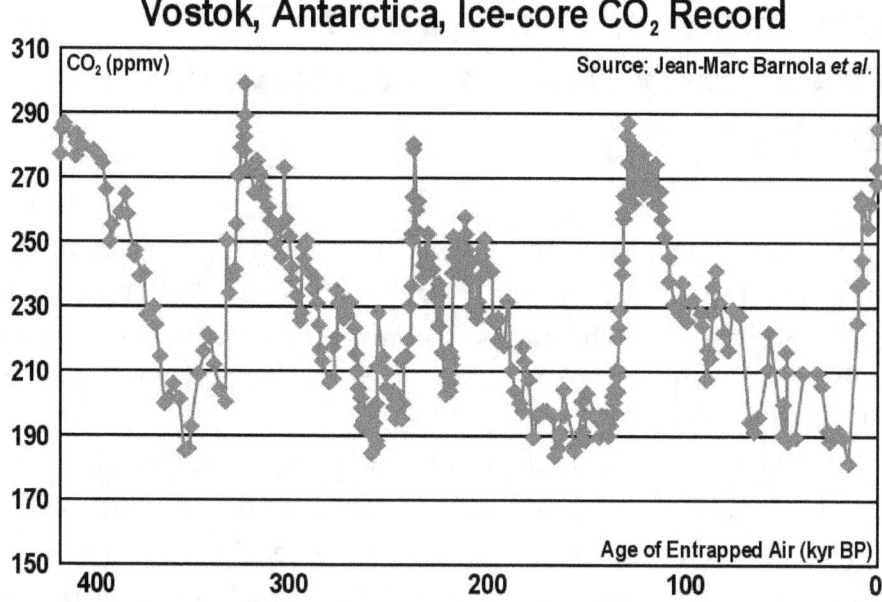

Vostok, Antarctica, Ice-core CO_2 Record

Because animals breathe out CO_2, they help to keep the level from going too low. But animals have a hard time living in the cold or desert climates so common during a glacial period. Of course, plants have an even harder time surviving such challenges. They cannot grow fur to protect themselves from the cold. In the ice, they hibernate. They essentially shut down during cold periods. And during a glacial period, the temperate zones are, for the most part, in permanent winter—for 90,000 years.

Lightning strikes and volcanoes can also increase CO_2 content. But if something were to kill off most, or all of the animals—like some pathogen—plants could more quickly use up the existing atmospheric CO_2. Weathering of silicate rocks also tends to draw down CO_2 over geologically long periods of time. Inexorably, the path for CO_2 has long been toward the extinction of life. Humans have interrupted this trend. Extinction from CO_2 starvation has been put on hold, thanks to humans burning so much fossil fuel.

If the cold of the glacial period were to deepen, then the oceans would soak up more CO_2 from the atmosphere, further reducing the partial pressure of carbon dioxide. This could happen because of volcanic aerosols or other impediments to insolation (sunshine on the Earth's surface). This could also occur if the solar wind were to die down. This would allow far more cosmic rays to strike the Earth, generating far more clouds, further cooling our world (Mortensen, 2008).

During the 1816, year without a summer, volcanic aerosols from Mount Tambora, Dutch East Indies (modern Indonesia), surrounded the planet, across the northern hemisphere, and reduced the global average temperature by as much as 1°C cooler. This much cooling ended up killing thousands of people.

Compare this volcanic event to the last glacial period. The depths of that cold era of the current Ice Age were as much as 10–11°C cooler than today. A prolonged period of such deep cooling could make the oceans even colder, and make them more hungry to take in additional carbon dioxide. This could plunge the plant world into a "Red Line" stupor, triggering multiple extinctions.

The Fuzzy Red Line

Most boundaries in nature are not precise, hard lines. There's typically a lot of messy fuzziness around the edges. Snow in the northern regions doesn't always arrive on the same day every year. The "edge" of snow season is thus fuzzy.

The beginning of the Holocene was somewhat arbitrary. Do we measure from the start of the initial warm-up? Do we start from when the first warming trend reached its earliest peak? Or do we measure from the end of the Younger Dryas cold period which interrupted the far warmer, interglacial climate?

Some of the earlier interglacials barely warmed enough to reach the coldest levels of our current interglacial. Though they were far warmer than the Ice Age glacial periods on either side of the time scale, they remained far cooler than the Holocene. So, even the extent of warming is fuzzy. The amplitude of that interglacial warmth varies greatly.

Likewise, our current interglacial has remained far cooler than the Eemian at its peak. In fact, according to Vostok ice core data, the Eemian had a stretch of about 4,000 years that never got colder than our warmest periods in the Holocene—including the Holocene Optimum (Archive.org).

These variations make the definition of interglacial somewhat more fuzzy. The beginning point of our current Ice Age is also equally arbitrary.

The figure 150 ppm for CO_2 was first posed by Lovelock and Whitfield in their 1982 letter to *Nature* magazine. At that level, C3 species start to have difficulty utilizing CO_2 in photosynthesis. But it's not a hard line. Many C3 species can still utilize CO_2 down to 50 or 60 ppm. Below that level, they die.

C4 species, however, can utilize CO_2 down nearly to zero. Such conditions would result in far smaller plants with far less nutritional value. Animals could be forced to over-graze and drive such plants into extinction from simple herbivory.

C3 Plant Species

The older species (C3), more sensitive to CO_2 shortages, include, wheat, spinach, apple, coffee, sugar beet, tobacco, barley, rice, mango, oat, soybean, peanut, bean, potato, cotton, most lawn grasses (fescue, rye and Kentucky bluegrass), the majority of trees (including evergreen trees) and many shrubs (tropics to Mediterranean). In the wild, 85% of all plant species are C3 types (CropsReview.com).

All of these species would suffer greatly from CO_2 levels below 150 ppm, and some would die. Below 50 ppm all remaining C3 species would die.

Imagine a world with no more apples, breads, pastas, rice, mangos, oats, soy, peanuts, beans, potatoes, asparagus, bananas, berries, carrots, broccoli, chilies and peppers, oranges, lemons, limes, coffee, coconuts, hops (for making beer), lettuce, melons, olives, onions, papayas, peas, pumpkins, squashes, sweet potatoes, yams or cotton (Sage and Zhu). Imagine a world where many species of trees, shrubs and lawn grasses no longer exist. All of these C3 species require more than 50 ppm CO_2. As we'll discover in the next chapter, some C3 species freaked out when CO_2 levels dropped below 800 ppm (twice today's starvation levels).

C4 Plant Species

The newer species, less sensitive to CO_2 shortages, include, maize (American corn), sugarcane, amaranth and many desert plants. C4 plants make up only about 3% of land plant species. According to CropsReview.com, grasses and sedges "comprise roughly 79% of the total number of C4 species." Many types of weeds are also C4—nutgrass, bermuda grass, goose-grass, common purslane, crabgrass, pigweed, itchgrass, plus tumbleweed (Russian thistle).

While we may be able to survive on maize, sugarcane and a few other food crops, these greatly restrict our nutritional choices.

CAM Plant Species

A third type of plant species has capabilities intermediate to those of C3 and C4 species. These are largely desert plants, like cacti. These include about 8% of land plant species. However, pineapple is the only CAM crop of any significance (Georgia State University).

During a glacial period, when rain becomes far more scarce, these types of plants are more certain to survive than C3 plants.

Bravo, Humans!

If humans had not burned fossil fuels during the current interglacial, the outlook for plants in the next glacial period would have been much more dire. Without the extra CO_2 from fossil fuel burning, Earth's atmosphere could conceivable have reached the "Red Line" and eventually ended all life on Earth.

So, we need to be thankful to our fellow humans for accidentally saving all life on Earth. Of course it wasn't intentional, but we should at least be aware that it happened.

In the online forums, I occasionally run across some individual who condemns humans for ruining the planet. Quite often they will say something like, "Humans should stop having children," or "I'll be glad if humans go extinct." We have to wonder, if they hate their human kind so much, why they remain alive. While suicide is the most selfish thing one can do, it remains hypocritical for them to wish human life dead while remaining alive. Their comments seem to serve no purpose other than making others apathetic.

We can remain aware of such emotionally conflicted conditions, but our focus needs to be on the more positive picture—helping humanity and all life thrive. Most humans contribute to nature. Some don't. We need to know the difference. The human corporation, for instance, is based on the simple principle of selfishness. Every action a corporation takes is calculated to return profits to their owners. By itself, profit is not a bad thing. Ironically, this selfishness frequently works against the best interests of their customers. This is a fact that many are only now beginning to realize.

Perhaps we can take some solace in our accidental heroism. Hooray for humans. Thank you all for helping to save life on Earth from death by carbon dioxide starvation. Thank you all for burning fossil fuels. Now, we need to find cleaner ways to do more of that.

And we need to be kind to all Third World citizens by allowing them to attain prosperity, too. By burning fossil fuels, they will be helping to improve our world. Admittedly, this sounds strange after so many years of hearing carbon dioxide condemned in the media. But the lies have persisted too long. It's time to "clear the air."

Chapter 2 — CO₂ Starvation

The "Red Line" of death isn't the only problem with carbon dioxide levels. A little over thirty million years ago, when CO_2 levels had dropped below about 800 ppm, plants began freaking out. They ended up evolving C4 species to cope with the CO_2 starvation. But think about this for a moment. That starvation level—800 ppm—was twice what carbon dioxide levels are today (~400 ppm).

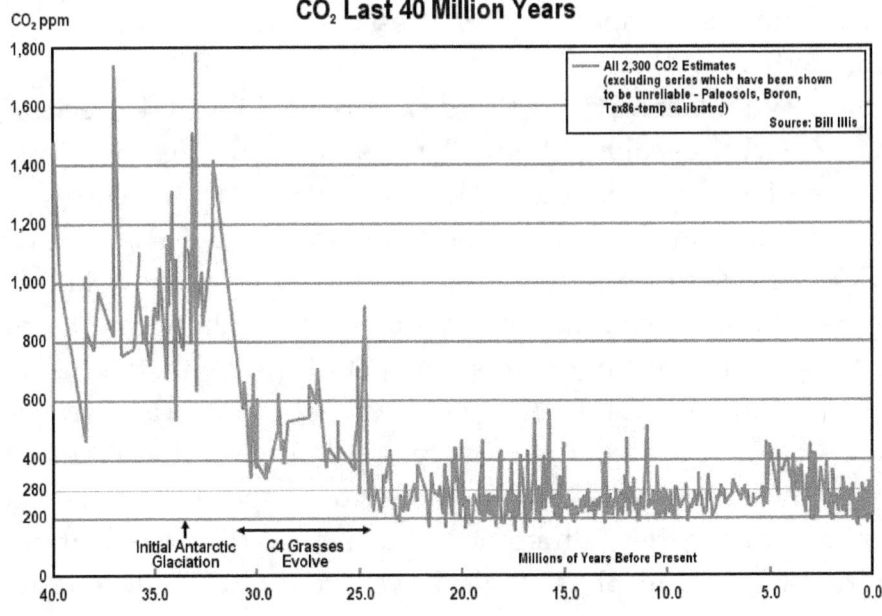

CO₂ Last 40 Million Years

If you are starving on one bowl of rice per day, and then you have to cut back to half a bowl of rice per day, that's double the starvation. I seriously doubt if the effects are entirely linear, though. Lower nutrition levels would tend to exacerbate the body's inability to heal from disease or injury. The body needs nutrients just to exist. If nutrition levels are cut back too far, then the body has nothing left for other functions—like healing, fighting off disease or simple tasks to improve the chances of survival. I suspect all life is like this.

Gerhart and Ward state, "[CO_2] has varied throughout geologic time, and during some periods may have been so low as to greatly limit plant growth and reproduction." They go on to point out that, "From the studies that have been conducted, it is clear that modern C3 plant genotypes grown at low [CO_2] (180–200 ppm) exhibit severe reductions in photosynthesis, survival, growth, and reproduction, suggesting that reduced [CO_2] during glacial periods may have induced carbon limitations that would have been highly stressful on C3 plants.... In addition, carbon limitations at low [CO_2] may have altered plant tolerance ranges to other stressors such as drought, heat, and herbivory."

What Gerhart and Ward say about C3 vs. C4 species is particularly revealing about plants' abilities to deal with low levels of carbon dioxide. "The author found that corn and sugar cane (now known to be C4 plants) could draw down [CO_2] below 10 ppm, whereas the other species (now known to be C3 plants) could only draw down [CO_2] between 60 and 145 ppm. Interestingly, this low-[CO_2] study distinguished plants with the C4 vs C3 photosynthetic pathways several years before the formal discovery of C4 photosynthesis. At the time, the author was unable to provide a specific mechanism to account for these differences, but realized he was working with two unique physiological systems. It was later shown that C4 plants have a CO$_2$ compensation point that is close to 0 ppm, whereas that of C3 plants is in the vicinity of 50–60 ppm between 25 and 30°C."

During photosynthesis, a biochemical molecule known as RuBisCO (ribulose-1,5-bisphosphate carboxylase/oxygenase), acts as a catalyst to fix CO$_2$—in other words, remove it from the atmosphere and incorporate it into a solid. When the ratio of CO$_2$ to oxygen gets too low, the C3 plant suffers a major problem. "Photorespiration is increased at low [CO$_2$] because both CO$_2$ and O$_2$ compete for the same active site of Rubisco. A reduction in [CO$_2$]/[O$_2$] enhances oxygenation, resulting in carbon loss to the plant." In other words, instead of a plant fixing CO$_2$, it begins to fix oxygen.

C4 Species

There are about 7,600 species of plants that utilize the C4 method of carbon dioxide acquisition—called "carbon fixation." All of these plant species are angiosperms, or flowering plants. These include many food crops like sugar cane, sorghum, maize (American corn), and millet. Many grasses are also C4. Many grains like rice and wheat are C3 and remain far more susceptible to CO$_2$ starvation.

Scientists have begun genetic development of C4 rice, which is normally only a C3 species. It proves quite ironic that they would be committing such an effort to creating a version of rice that can withstand greater CO$_2$ starvation in an era when humans are generating more beneficial CO$_2$. Part of this irony can be traced back to the misconception that CO$_2$ is bad. Perhaps they are counting on governments sequestering more of this vital substance and deepening the CO$_2$ starvation plants are already suffering.

An End to CO$_2$ Starvation?

What if we were to continue increasing CO$_2$ content in the atmosphere? As we'll see in the coming chapters, global warming is remarkably good. Ironically, carbon dioxide has very little to do with that warming. It would be nice if it did, because then we could have some control over Earth's thermostat. But there are a great many pieces of evidence which show that CO$_2$ is simply not the cause of our modern warming. Its contribution to that warming remains small.

But think what the extra CO$_2$ would mean for plants. One major effect on plants is that the C3 species become better able to withstand harsher conditions, especially low-water environments. This would mean that deserts would become "endangered" by life encroaching on its dead territory. In other words, deserts would become semi-deserts. And what's wrong with relatively lifeless areas becoming threatened by life? Shouldn't we become concerned for the person who tries to protect lifeless, barren land? As an artist, I can understand the desire to preserve a certain look. But if we take lots of photographs and paint paintings before life overtakes those dead landscapes, then the look will be preserved. Let life take over.

A live leaf is far more valuable than a dead rock. Let's promote more life. Let's increase our fossil fuel burning, but make it cleaner.

Chapter 3 — What More CO$_2$ Means

If carbon dioxide is an essential gas for plant life, could more CO$_2$ prove beneficial to plant growth? The answer is a resounding, "Yes!"

In fact, modern increases in CO$_2$ have been greening the Earth for years. Marginal lands have become more filled with life. Existing greenery have increased their foliage. Deserts are starting to "suffer" the encroachment of life. Ironically, the so-called "green" environmentalists don't like this. In a very real sense, they have become "global greening deniers." While I dislike the use of such *ad hominem* verbiage, I couldn't resist poking fun at the Warming Alarmists and their penchant for overly simplistic labels.

But is the extra green a good thing? Is life ever good? One Warming Alarmist website goes so far as to criticize this greening for the problems it creates on grazing animals because the brush is becoming thicker (Painting). Yes, they're complaining that life is actually benefiting. In fact, their website header artwork includes the picture of a penguin standing on snow, shocked that a sprig of green is poking up through the ice. They treat life as "horrifying." They may not say this, explicitly, but their subtext seems to shout it. Why would plant life supplanting dead, snow-ridden lands be a bad thing? Does someone there have an ice fetish?

In the realm of food production environments, green-house operators have known for quite some time that by pumping in more CO_2, their crop yields increase markedly. They make more profit, because the fruits and vegetables produced are larger and more plentiful.

Clearly, plants love it. But how about animals?

Currently, CO_2 is a trace gas in our atmosphere. It has something like 400 ppm (parts per million). That amounts to 0.04% or 0.0004 of the whole atmosphere. Tiny!

Humans can take far larger concentrations of CO_2. According to one website, the "maximum allowed concen-tration within a 8 hour working period: 5,000–10,000 ppm" (EngineeringToolBox.com). They also say that, "slightly intoxicating, breathing and pulse rate increase, nausea: 30,000–40,000 ppm."

NASA has set the spacecraft maximum allowable concentration (SMAC) for CO_2 at 20,000 ppm (15 mmHg) for periods of an hour or less (Law, Watkins, *et al*). For a 24-hour period, the SMAC has been set at 13,000 ppm (10 mmHg). For 7–180 days, SMAC is 7,000 ppm (5 mmHg). And the new SMAC for 1,000-day missions is 5,000 ppm (3.8 mmHg). So, the range for astronauts on the space station, for instance, or a mission to Mars, is between 5,000–20,000 ppm (12.5–50 times the current atmospheric concentration).

U.S. Navy submarines have set their maximum CO_2 level at 8,000 ppm (James and Macatangay). This is 20 times the current CO_2 levels in the atmosphere.

So, humans can take on up to 10,000 ppm carbon dioxide without dire health effects. That's 25 times the current, ambient level in our atmosphere. Humans can go from regular ambient air breathing to a submarine environment in seconds without suffering any significant problems.

The average CO$_2$ level for the last 600 million years was something like 1,600 ppm (conservative)—4 times the current level. Life remembers. This is the environment in which life evolved. As we've already seen, 800 ppm was about the level of CO$_2$ starvation strong enough to initiate planet-wide evolution of C4 species in order to cope with the carbon dioxide starvation. Were plants uncomfortable at higher levels? This remains a possibility. And we're faced with the question: What is the optimal level of CO$_2$ for plants? Have modern plants evolved away from higher CO$_2$ levels, or do they still hunger for more of the "good stuff?" More research needs to be done on this point, but we already have some research that points to far higher levels as the desired environment.

Carbon Dioxide Limits

All gases have their limits, including oxygen. According to one study by the Rand Corporation in the 60s, the maximum oxygen content for one atmosphere of pressure is 56%—560,000 ppm. Above this point, the body starts to react adversely to what is called "oxygen toxicity."

As we've seen, humans can tolerate 10,000 ppm CO$_2$ without dire consequences.

Every species has their own sensitivities. Some plants produce more up to 2,000 ppm, while some experience a slight decrease in productivity above 1,000 ppm. Likely, there won't be a perfect CO$_2$ level for all species. So, when the corporate news media tells us that one plant species will suffer at certain levels of carbon dioxide, we have to take that with the proverbial grain of salt. Other species will likely benefit more.

Perhaps we could all agree on the average CO$_2$ level for the last 600 million years. After all, that is the level around

which all species evolved. If we home in on this average—
1,600 ppm—those species which remember will "breathe a
sigh of relief," and those which came later, like the C4 species,
can adapt.

Very likely, we don't need to get much higher than
1,600 ppm with CO_2 levels, but it would be gratifying to move
the levels further from the deadly "Red Line" of carbon
dioxide extinction levels.

Chapter 4 — How Fast is Too Fast?

Most, if not all plants in a greenhouse respond immediately — favorably. This is up to 1,000 ppm above our current ambient levels; i.e. 1,400 ppm. People have no problem with CO_2 levels up to 8,000 ppm, like on naval submarines. That's for land-based life.

Now, if we're talking oceans, global warming is actively reducing the rate of CO_2 absorption. Warmer water cannot hold as much carbon dioxide. In fact, part of the modern increases in CO_2 are from ocean outgassing caused by our wonderful global warming. This puts the plans of governments to cool down the planet into a new perspective. By cooling the planet, they would be making the state of the oceans far worse by reducing their temperatures. That would force more CO_2 back into the water, greatly exacerbating any problems of ocean pH.

Continuing our warming helps ocean species have more time to adapt to increasing CO_2 levels.

Temperature Rates

Rising temperature is similarly benign. Take for instance the daily "torture" of Los Angeles citizens who have to endure an average daily warming of 20.8°F (11.6°C) in November. In May, the average daily warming is a bit less at 17.4°F (9.7°C). These are merely average, and range from more than three times to nearly four times the UN's horror story of 3°C warming over the next century. People and animals in Los Angeles have no problem adapting to far greater temperature swings on a daily basis. This notion is nonsense that species are going to keel over dead with a 0.03°C of warming every year. I doubt if there is a species on Earth that can feel that small a change in global average temperature. Yet, the daily temperature swings make this minuscule amount of global average warming look like nothing. Individual species, locally, won't notice it.

As far as species adapting to changes in climate, if Earth were to warm by +3°C over the next century, the mid-latitude climate would effectively be moved about 200 kilometers farther north. A turtle could crawl that distance in a few months and wait the remainder of the UN's "century of terror" (Martin, 2016 video).

Scary? Of course not! Even a turtle can outrun the UN's supposed disaster.

Chapter 5 — Global Warming and the Start of Civilization

Did you know that global warming made civilization possible?

At the end of the last glacial period of the current Ice Age—about 13,500 BC, global temperatures shot up as much as +7°C in 50 years. This is nearly five times the UN's scare story of +3°C per century (+1.5°C per 50 years). This could have started civilization, but nature pulled the rug out from under this early warming attempt. Scientists believe a large spill of fresh ice water from North American glacial melt caused the shutdown of the Atlantic Ocean's thermohaline circulation. This put a cap of lighter, fresh water on top of the denser salt water. This began a 1,300-year "Big Freeze" known as the Younger Dryas. We are likely not to see a repeat of this from Greenland melting, for two reasons. Greenland's ice cap is too small, and there is no place for glacial melt to collect for a massive spill at a later date. Most Greenland melt goes immediately to the ocean, spreading the cold, fresh water spill over a longer period of time—plenty of time to mix with the denser salt water.

Global temperatures during this return to glacial conditions (Younger Dryas) still went up and down, but centered at a much colder level. Then, about 9600 BC, the Younger Dryas abruptly ended. Something broke through the cap on the thermohaline circulation. Within 50 years, temperatures had rebounded as much as +5°C. This is huge on a global scale. That's a rate of +10°C per century.

The End of Another Civilization?

Ironically, something big happened about 9600 BC that coincided with the sudden end to the Younger Dryas. The nominal date for the end of the "Big Freeze" has been pegged by some sources at 9620 BC, plus-or-minus a few decades. In the Greenland GISP2 ice cores, traces were found of volcanic residue at 9620.77 BC (NOAA). So, somewhere in the world, just before that date, there was a moderately large volcanic eruption—VEI 5–7 (volcanic explosivity index). A 1989 article in *Nature* magazine provided information on 17,000 years of sea level rise (Fairbanks). On the graph accompanying that article, there was a 2-meter drop right at the end of the Younger Dryas. While this could have been the product of errors in measurement, or noise in the data, it could also have been a real artifact—a proxy for a subsidence, or tectonic collapse, somewhere in the oceans of Earth. More corroboration is needed.

So, we have three major events occurring at the same time—approximately 9620 BC—which suggest that something big happened at that time.

- A sudden break in the thermohaline cap which had held the Younger Dryas "Big Freeze" in place (something may have vigorously stirred up the Atlantic Ocean),
- A major volcanic eruption somewhere in the world, and
- A sudden drop in sea level of approximately 2 meters.

There is a fourth event which coincides with these three, but scientists have dismissed it as "fantasy." This is none other than Plato's Atlantis sinking approximately 9600 BC.

In my upcoming book, *Mission: Atlantis,* I will describe the science behind validating the possibility of Atlantis. Though none of these elements prove Atlantis, they keep open the door to its possible past existence.

It should seem ironic to any student of science that any scientist would claim that Atlantis did not exist because there is no evidence of its existence. Such is an argument to ignorance logical fallacy. For one thing, they haven't looked! That's bad enough. We have some evidence. But a further irony comes from the fact that they refuse to look for any other, new evidence. This reveals a political nature to the topic—plus an emotional one. Scientists *fear* to look because it might jeopardize their careers.

The same "disease" has struck climate scientists, medical doctors and anyone else who might lose their jobs from talking about unpopular topics or from entertaining unpopular viewpoints. It behooves all of us to remain cordial and humble when someone else provides evidence that disagrees with our own world view. How else are we to learn—especially if we are to learn that we are wrong? In 2012, I learned to swallow ego on a number of topics. It proved to be difficult, but not impossible. The pain ego suffers is temporary; the pain from mistakes of science, and the policy based on those mistakes, can prove to be deadly for millions or even billions of people.

Effects on the Environment

But with all that global warming happening 12,000 years ago, what were the effects on the environment? What happened besides melting a lot more ice far more quickly? What was it that made civilization possible?

In order to understand this rather simple phenomenon, we have to unlearn something with which the news media has been haranguing us for more than a decade. What is this lie? The Warming Alarmists claim that global warming will increase deserts and droughts. (Paradoxically, they also say it will increase flooding, too, but that's a different topic altogether.)

Ask yourself: How does land ever get water? Of course, land gets water from rain. There are no other significant sources. Irrigation comes from rain (or from that frozen rain we call snow). But where does rain come from? Clouds, of course, and clouds come from excess water vapor, and water vapor comes from evaporation of the oceans. Evaporation, my fellow humans, comes from warming of the oceans. You can't get much rain from cold oceans. Global warming will increase rain, and decrease deserts and droughts. Some of that rain will inevitably spill over into drier lands.

If you've been a Warming Alarmist like I was, this may be making you dizzy about now. I went through this stage, too, and it will pass. Part of what you may be feeling is the sense that you've been lied to. And you're right. You have. Get over it.

Global warming made civilization possible by making rain far more common. With more rain, came the possibility of agriculture. Before the massive global warming at the start of the Holocene interglacial, agriculture was simply not possible in most locations on the planet. There wasn't enough rain.

Thermal Gradients, Turbulence, and Storms

Through it all, the tropics have not changed much. They have remained at largely the same average temperature during Ice Age and non-Ice Age periods. Our interglacial is Ice Age material, but somewhat warmer than the glacial periods. Despite the relatively steady temperatures, the tropics were far from idyllic paradises during the periods of huge ice sheets.

With the massive cooling which plunges the world into a glacial period, polar cold is moved far closer to equatorial heat. During the last glacial period, the North American ice sheet came as far south as Kansas. What happens when you put ice into the fire? Imagine for a moment, placing a large ice cube onto a white-hot chunk of iron or tungsten. The ice quickly melts. On the surface of that melt, the water is quickly turned to steam, boiling away in moments. The change is energetic and perhaps even violent. Now, pour a similar quantity of cool water onto a warm slab of steel. Not much happens. The water flows off of the surface, if it's flat. What little water remains evaporates in short order. But there are no sparks, and no flashes of explosive boiling. The temperature difference is what causes the energetic response.

During a glacial period of the current Ice Age, the extreme thermal gradient, between the ice and equatorial heat, generates far stronger and more frequent storms. This temperature difference is where storms get all of their energy.

We don't have any storm records from the last glacial period. Writing had not yet been invented. Human population levels had been constrained by the cold to a few tens of thousands, according to modern estimates.

The work of Hubert H. Lamb, the initial director of the Climate Research Unit at East Anglia University, shows us that the Little Ice Age was far stormier than the warm periods on either side (Lamb). The 13th century, in particular, was racked by storm surges and flooding devastating the coastal regions of Western and Northern Europe. Two storms during the Little Ice Age have gained some notoriety. In 1588, a massive storm off the coast of England sank much of the Spanish Armada, saving England from becoming a Spanish speaking nation. The Great Storm of 1703 brought hurricane force winds to the ports of England, wrecking the economy that year. England doesn't usually get hurricanes.

But if you warm up the poles and melt all the ice, you have little or no thermal gradient and the source of energy all but disappears. The poles will naturally remain cooler, so some milder wind will continue to blow, but there will be far fewer storms, if any.

The tropics, during a glacial period, will receive far more punishment from storms. Attempting to grow crops or to start civilization, there, would likely prove to be impossible. Any infrastructure established one year, could easily be destroyed the next. The tropics during an interglacial, like our current Holocene, prove to be far more calm. If the Ice Age were to end, the tropics would become even more calm and idyllic.

Remove the thermal gradient, and storms disappear. Without their energy source, they cannot exist.

Global Warming Benefits

When global warming started off the Holocene interglacial, storms suddenly had far less energy than they did during the last glacial period. In fact, during the 20th century warming period, storm counts have dropped dramatically. The NOAA data on strong tornadoes (EF3–EF5) show a 60-year downtrend, from the earliest date on the graph. The data from Dr. Ryan Maue on tropical cyclones (hurricanes and typhoons), shows a similar downtrend for counts as well as accumulated cyclone energy (ACE). There has been a lot of up and down, but the trend is clear. Total global hurricane frequency dropped from about 66 in 1971 to 48 in 2015. Accumulated Cyclone Energy (104 knots2) shows a trend from a little over 1,500 in 1972 to under 1,400 in 2014 for global values. For northern hemisphere, values range from 1,200 in 1972 to a little over 900 in 2014 (Maue).

Of course, there is a great deal of up and down on modern climate graphs. We can expect a broad range of natural variability within any short span of time. But the principles of physics remain the same. If you cut the source of energy, you reduce or eliminate the existence of storms. And the source of energy for storms is temperature difference. Storms won't disappear overnight, and the number of storms will continue to go up and down whether we experience global warming or global cooling.

The combination of three factors helped to make civilization possible:
- Warmth, which promotes life (including human life),
- Rain, which promotes agriculture, and
- Relative calm, which allows for the establishment of infrastructure.

But global warming came with one other benefit. Because warm water doesn't hold as much carbon dioxide, the enormous global warming at the start of the Holocene forced massive amounts of CO_2 out of the oceans, making plants healthier and more productive. Agriculture, which had been relatively impossible before the Holocene, suddenly had all the ingredients it needed—warmth, water, and carbon dioxide.

Human population started to pull away from the meager tens of thousands, which had persisted throughout the glacial period, and eventually made it up to the millions and now billions.

Certainly there's a limit on the number of people the planet will support, but we're not even close to that limit. With proper management, this world could support several hundred billion people. With off-planet resources, like food from Venus and mining from the asteroids, we might even support population levels into the trillions. However, population levels tend to stabilize when a culture has prosperity. Japan even has a negative population growth. So, any talk about there being too many people on Earth could be merely dangerous propaganda meant to make murder or genocide look reasonable.

Chapter 6 — Scorched Earth Fantasy

Many years ago, I could not believe the news that some enterprising customer had sued McDonalds for serving hot coffee without letting her know that it was "hot." It seemed ironic that she won. That seemed to be one of the low points in legal history. My own outrage was a misconception perpetrated by corporations to demonize an elderly woman who was nearly killed by coffee that was far hotter than most of us would make at home. Do people file frivolous lawsuits? Sometimes. The case of Liebeck v. McDonalds doesn't seem to be one of them, despite how the news and other corporations portray the incident (Retro Report).

Sometimes corporations are forced to state the obvious —"coffee is hot." Getting the government or lawyers involved is hardly a good idea. But corporations tend to be selfish and self-centered, lacking any compassion. Whenever they seem to do "good," it is always something that will enhance their bottom line. Always. All too often, enhancing their bottom line includes a lot of evil. The popular misperception of the case— "woman scores $2.9 million over spilled coffee"—misses the fact that she tried to settle for far less and McDonalds refused to help her with her extensive medical bills and life-threat-ening injury. Personally, I like hot coffee, but not as hot as the big chains make it. I always have to cool it down before drinking.

Our perception of events like the McDonald's Coffee Case can be distorted by corporate disregard of facts. A similar fantasy about heat has been borne out of the climate debate.

On one of my YouTube videos, a visitor remarked that warming Scandinavia enough to become tropical would scorch the lower latitudes. He implied that people would die in droves, and plants and animals would not be able to survive the far warmer temperatures. Earth would become scorched.

I attempted to explain the non-linear nature of climate. However, the image that had been pounded into his psyche could not be dislodged by facts, logic, analogy or any other device of reason.

During the last glacial period, the tropics were virtually the same as they are today, except perhaps a bit more violent from the high-thermal gradient storms. After all, ice brought closer to heat jacks up the temperature differential, generating far more energy for storm creation.

When the Holocene started, global average temper-atures shot up, but the tropics barely budged. They became a little calmer, but still received the occasional cyclone. Why do the tropics experience so little difference in temperature? Why would Al Gore be right about this in his documentary, *An Inconvenient Truth?* In that paradoxically award-winning film, Gore stated that a +5° of global warming would result in very little equatorial warming, but a whopping +12° of warming at the poles. Most of his other facts were misleading or down-right wrong.

Would it surprise you to find out that our planet has a nifty temperature regulator? It's called water. It can be found in our oceans. It helps to keep temperatures from swinging too far one way or the other. In fact, during the entire history of our planet, the global average temperature has varied less than 5%. That's amazingly steady for nearly 4.5 billion years of climate change.

Here's how it works.

There are a number of natural factors which force temperature to go up, and other factors which force temperature to go down. The result is a kind of equilibrium between all forces. It is the resultant vector of all input vectors.

The sun shines on our planet in the visible light spectrum. This is electromagnetic radiation which passes right through the atmosphere as if it weren't even there. To these frequencies, the gases of the atmosphere remain transparent. However, light striking a surface warms up that surface. The darker the surface, the more it absorbs the higher frequency visible light and converts it into lower frequency infrared radiation—sometimes called "heat" radiation. Some of the gases in our atmosphere are relatively opaque to these lower frequencies. These are called the greenhouse gases. Unlike a glass greenhouse, the atmosphere does not have hard surfaces. The absorption of infrared and reemission of those same wavelengths takes place throughout the vertical atmosphere. Scientists only talk about an "optical thickness" or layers in the atmosphere as a convenience in discussing a process which is far from digital in nature.

Warming ocean waters excite the water molecules and some escape the liquid state to become water vapor—the gaseous state. During this process, called evaporation, energy is transferred from the surrounding water surface to the now gaseous molecule. This we sense as evaporative cooling.

Stacking up the various greenhouse gases against one another, water vapor does the lion's share of the warming effect—the greenhouse blanket. Even though each molecule of water vapor is less effective than a molecule of CO_2, there is so much more water vapor than carbon dioxide. Water vapor does about 95% of the greenhouse heavy lifting. Methane is even more potent than carbon dioxide, molecule-for-molecule, but methane is even more rare than CO_2. And methane is highly flammable. This means that any flame or lightning strike will burn up adjacent methane. This is one of the reasons methane can never build up in our atmosphere, no matter how many cows are passing gas.

But water has another trick up its molecular "sleeve." It's called clouds. Water vapor condenses in the upper atmosphere to become clouds. And thick, low clouds reflect sunlight back into space before it ever has a chance to heat up the surface. This produces an additional cooling effect. This is why the UN's IPCC keeps getting their climate models all wrong (Watts, 2013). Their predictions continue to run far too hot, because they don't include these potent negative feedbacks from Earth's temperature regulator.

Both of these effects keep the tropics from runaway warming. Higher latitudes don't experience as much evaporative cooling, which is a good thing. They don't need as much.

Global Warming Causes Extinctions?

One claim that seems to rear its head quite often during climate debates is the notion that global warming is causing all manner of species extinctions. When Warming Alarmists are asked to name 10 species, they cannot. When asked to name 5, they attempt to change the subject. When they mention 1 species that was hunted to extinction, they cannot provide a plausible link to global warming. Even polar bears are doing quite well with more food. Seal populations have gone up, so bears are getting fat, and their numbers have increased. Some bears are also learning to get food from other sources.

Even the IPCC admitted that global warming cannot be linked to the extinction of any species (Watts, 2014).

The Real Results of Global Warming and Melting the Polar Ice

With enough global warming to melt all the polar ice, the tropics may warm up a tiny amount, but they will be increasingly more calm. There may still be storms, but they will become more rare and weaker overall. You cannot have storms when their source of energy ceases to exist.

The desert regions will shrink in size and become deeper, harder deserts—more dry—where they do persist. During the far warmer Holocene Optimum, the Sahara became green for up to 5,000 years (Manning).

Can we expect more deserts to behave this way? That remains unknown. It will depend on local weather, including new monsoon patterns.

Temperate zones will increase in size, but they will lose much of the deep seasonality of winter cold. Some of the temperate zone may still see snow, but it will become increasingly rare. The ice regions will disappear and give up their tortured lands to life. Polar bears will shed some of their fur, and adjust to the warmer climate. Penguins and seals will also adjust. Life adapts.

Will we ever have scorching temperatures? Yes, more than likely, but these will probably be constrained to the deserts where the ameliorating effects of water's temperature regulator cannot be felt.

The only significantly negative effect of global warming will be sea level rise. The lands lost along the coasts will be replaced by lands formerly buried by ice or locked in permafrost. But even there, global warming slows down the rate of sea level rise. How? Because it generates more evaporation from the oceans and this water vapor is converted to snow and trapped at the poles. The net effect is to slow down the rate of sea level rise, giving us more time to move (Mortensen, 2004).

If we were to melt all the ice, we would be inconvenienced by having to move. If we don't melt all the ice, and the next glacial period grips the Earth with far more of the white stuff, billions would be inconvenienced to death. Big difference. Cold kills; warmth promotes life.

Future Scorched Earth?

Our sun is not constant. Ever since it was born, roughly 4.5 billion years ago, it has become brighter and brighter. The change has remained very gradual. There have also been minor fluctuations, up and down, in the sun's visible light output, but these are tiny. They can be disregarded for most calculations.

Every billion years, the sun increases in brightness about 10%. From the time of the dinosaurs (about 65 million years), the sun has brightened about 0.62% (more than half a percent). During that time, the atmosphere has lost a great deal of CO_2, which has helped to make the world a little cooler. But the levels of CO_2 are now so low, they currently have very little effect on the global climate. What little warmth they hold onto is almost entirely negated by Earth's temperature regulator—water's evaporative cooling and cloud shading.

Eventually, the Earth will have nothing to help keep it cool as the sun becomes increasingly warm. In another billion years, life on the surface will have a hard time surviving. In another 1.5 billion years, the oceans could start to boil. Water molecules in the upper atmosphere could become lost to the solar wind, depleting the Earth of its precious compound (Kollipara).

So, we have hundreds of millions of years yet to go, all other things being equal.

Chapter 7 — Global Warming and the End of Storms?

Have you ever felt the warmth coming off of an open flame? Have you ever seen the smoke rise from a candle? Have you ever experienced anything lightweight being blown into a fire from the side because of the updraft? Wind happens because of temperature differences.

When you move polar cold next to equatorial heat, you increase the thermal gradient, giving storms far more power. When you move polar cold farther from equatorial heat—or remove the ice altogether—then you decrease the potential for storms.

Numerous websites explain these simple principles, so it's not like people don't have access to the science basics. WeatherWizKids.com tells us that wind is "produced by the uneven heating of the earth's surface by the sun."

TheWeatherPrediction.com explains wind in terms of pressure differences, but clarifies, "The high and low pressure systems usually develop due to temperature differences. For this essay memorize this important concept: temperature differences result in pressure differences and this causes the air to move. This is true on all scales from the jet stream and low pressure systems to sea breeze circulations" (Haby). So, if you ever hear anyone claiming that it's pressure differences and *not* temperature differences that causes wind to blow, simply ask them, What causes the pressure differences?

NASA's SciJinks website also emphasizes this point: "The main cause of wind is a little surprising. It's actually **temperature.** More specifically, it's differences in temperature between different areas."

This is really a simple concept. It not only works in theory, it has been proven by modern measurements and empirical evidence.

The simple physics involved explains why the surface of Venus has had very little wind for millions of years. Many meteor craters on the surface of Earth's hot twin planet have remained pristine since they were created, several million years ago. There is no evidence of tornadoes or hurricanes. This should not be surprising, because the temperature on the surface of Venus is largely the same everywhere. Without a thermal difference to drive the hot, thick air on Venus, it would have no reason to move, except perhaps the occasional volcanic eruption or meteor impact.

This simple physics also explains why the extreme cold of Jupiter can host storms that are larger than our entire Earth. Those storms are incessant. They keep stirring up the clouds on the king of solar planets as they have done for billions of years. All it takes is a temperature difference—like the difference between super cold and moderately frozen. Any thermal gradient, no matter how cold can produce movement.

If we remove the temperature difference between poles and equator, we remove the battery pack which powers all storms. We probably don't want to go that far. We need some circulation. A little bit of wind is a good thing. But we don't need hurricanes and tornadoes.

Can we eliminate all dangerous storms? That is unknown. But by reducing the thermal gradient between poles and equator, we will certainly lose many of our yearly tropical cyclones and tornadoes.

Chapter 8 — Not Guilty!

Doesn't it feel good when an innocent victim of slander and wrongful accusations is cleared of all criminal charges?

Carbon dioxide is not guilty. It is too weak to account for global warming. How can we be so certain?

Not Guilty of Warming

First of all, paleoclimatic records show that Earth has experienced far warmer climate and far higher levels of CO_2 without going into runaway greenhouse warming. About the Cretaceous Thermal Maximum (~85–90 million years ago), Richard Norris wrote, "Sea surface temperature data...suggest that tropical temperatures exceeded 35°C. These temperatures were 5–7°C above those of the modern ocean, and high latitude temperatures were in the balmy mid 20°C range." That was for temperature. His team found evidence suggesting "the Cretaceous atmosphere must have had much higher-than-modern CO_2 levels—we predict concentrations of >4000 ppmv." That's ten times the current CO_2 concentration.

In other words, carbon dioxide is not the 800 pound gorilla the UN makes it out to be. Other factors are in control of the overall temperature of the planet. Even when the atmosphere had very little oxygen and something like 100,000 ppm of CO_2, our planet experienced an Ice Age. Oops! Sometimes it would be nice to have a tool—like carbon dioxide—for controlling the climate. But CO_2 is *not* such a tool, not at the concentrations of the last 600 million years.

During the Modern Warm Period, carbon dioxide has risen more-or-less steadily, but temperature has been up and down like crazy. The work of Svensmark, *et al*, has shown that clouds and cosmic ray influx far more closely track global average temperature (Mortensen). They have not yet proven a cause-and-effect relationship, but their research provides a far likelier suspect than carbon dioxide. CO_2 is disconnected when it comes to global average temperature. They are related, but only very weakly. It's like attempting to raise sea level by tossing a bucket of water into it. Such a bucket of water would have an effect, but it would remain immeasurable, because it's such a tiny amount.

The Holocene interglacial has had ten warm periods, based on Greenland ice cores (Humlum). That's one warm period every thousand years or so, except for a weak bump on a very high plateau of warmth about 4000 BC. Every other thousand-year period has had a strong peak of warmth surrounded by cooler climate on either side. That's ten natural warm periods; not nine natural and one human. To make matters worse, the presence of the Little Ice Age, plus a strong downward trend of warm period peaks for the last 3,000 years, shows that whatever effect humans have had on global warming has been weak, at best. In fact, the strong cooling of the last 3,000 years, suggests that the Holocene may already have started to shut down, preparing for the next glacial period.

Some Warming Alarmists will point out claims of "warmest year on record," and similar wording. What about these? We would have had a warm period with or without humans. Remember, we have had a warm period cycle every thousand years or so? Add to this the blatant fraud on the part of some scientists to lower old climate records and to raise more recent records in order to make any warming look more dramatic (Booker, Heller). This could also have been to eliminate any cooling or warming pause from the record (Cohen).

Add to this fraud the rather questionable retirement of hundreds of temperature stations in the United States resulting in a sharp spike in global average temperature on the very date of retirement (McKitrick). And add to this the rather awkward inclusion in post-retirement weather stations, monitoring units at places like asphalt parking lots (one in the Arizona desert), and standing right next to air conditioning exhaust vents (Watts). Hot, hot, hot! These stations not only take unrealistic advantage of the urban heat island effect, but also take advantage of the unnatural environment of asphalt and mechanical heat production. Ouch! At best, it's gross incompetence for scientists to be using this data. At worst, it could be premeditated fraud.

In January 2015, one reporter was able to get NASA scientists to confess that they were only 38% certain of their claim that 2014 was the warmest year on record. This was based on a margin of error (Rose). Oops, again!

Ironically, global warming is good, and the people who are trying so hard to convince us that it's bad are lying about the fact that it's happening at all. This ends up being a lie within a lie within a lie. Global warming is happening (not), is bad (not), and is caused by CO_2 (not).

Satellite data, which is the most thorough and most comprehensive data set of all temperature measuring methods on Earth, shows a substantial pause in global warming starting in 1998. That was the year of an El Niño event which significantly warmed things up. The year 2016 saw another El Niño event, but then global average temperature settled back down (Spencer).

There's no way to know whether or not we've reached the peak of this Modern Warm Period, but so far, the Modern remains cooler than the Medieval Warm Period which made Greenland farmable, and Northern England capable of growing grapes. The Medieval was cooler than the Roman Warm Period, and the Roman was cooler than the Minoan.

If CO_2 were such a powerhouse, then our Modern Warm Period should be standing tall amongst all warm periods. Instead, the Modern is the coolest of all 10 Holocene warm periods.

Global warming was the primary charge leveled against CO_2. We should be able to see, with all this evidence, that carbon dioxide is not guilty of causing the warming. But more importantly, we should see that global warming has never been a crime in the first place. So, for both reasons, carbon dioxide is not guilty.

Not Guilty of Pollution

Carbon dioxide has never been a pollutant, any more than oxygen is a pollutant. It remains a vital gas of life. The talk in the corporate mainstream media has included name-calling like "carbon" or "carbon pollution," as if we were talking about soot or something else dirty. Without this simple, vital, clean, odorless and harmless gas, we would not survive. All life on Earth would die.

If we had zero or near-zero oxygen in the atmosphere, all animals would die, but plants would still live with sufficient CO_2. On the other hand, if we had plenty of oxygen and zero carbon dioxide, all multicellular and most unicellular life would die—both plants and animals. First, plants would die, because of the lack of CO_2, then animals would die, because of the lack of food.

Not Guilty of "Ocean Acidification"

Does CO_2 change the pH of the ocean? Of course it does. But the oceans have seen far larger quantities of CO_2 and life thrived. The notion that increases in carbon dioxide are "acidifying" the ocean is misguided at best. You cannot make "more acidic" something that is not acidic in the first place. Oceans are alkaline. You can make them less alkaline, because they are already alkaline. This is more than a semantic distinction. People become emotional—even irrational—when you lie to them and slant the truth so that something is made to seem more dangerous.

Surprisingly, global warming is helping to solve the pH problem in the oceans.

Even if carbon dioxide levels have been much higher in the past, life in the oceans may need time to adapt. Well, guess what global warming does? It helps reduce the CO_2 in the oceans or to slow its accumulation! So, increasing CO_2 while warming the planet helps to alleviate the problems from ocean pH, and ocean life stress from pH changes. The levels of CO_2 dissolved in the ocean may increase, but only very slowly, because increasing warmth slows down the CO_2 absorption by the oceans, or may even reverse it. This, of course, depends on the rates of CO_2 production, and rates of warming.

Not Guilty, Not Guilty, Not Guilty

Any change will create problems. We need to step back from the topic as a whole and look at the bigger picture. Are the problems small which are being touted in the corporate mainstream media? Yes, very much so. Global *cooling* in an ongoing Ice Age is a far larger problem. Reducing CO_2 in a period of massive carbon dioxide starvation is also a far larger problem. Both of these problems could kill either billions of humans *or all life on the planet*. Global warming and increased CO_2 levels could jeopardize the crop yields of some species. Not such a big deal! Global warming could cause some people to move—including me! Again, not such a big deal.

So, congratulations carbon dioxide. You've been vindicated. Your role as a vital gas of life has been restored.

Chapter 9 — Hooray for Humans, but Watch Out for Corporations (and their owners)

Humans have saved all life on Earth by burning fossil fuels. This doesn't excuse the real pollution from sulfur dioxide, atrazine, glyphosate and thousands of other toxins. We still need to do more to protect the environment. But warmth and carbon dioxide are essential ingredients for life.

Like most true environmentalists, I want to have a clean planet, free of garbage-strewn panoramas, toxic chemical streams, and ruined soils chock full of carcinogenic compounds.

Humans have stumbled into saving all life on Earth. Hooray for humans. But accidental goodness is no excuse for lazy arrogance about the real problems facing us. We need to stop thinking we know it all and to remain open to all voices of dissent. We need to stop depending solely on experts, because sometimes experts can be bought off. Some Climate Realists also promote toxic pollution, because they work for corporations. And when the very avenue of discovery—the corporate news media and science journals are owned by the same people who want to pervert and control the dialog, we need to look hard for other sources of information.

The illusion of consensus on climate science makes it seem that a few lone voices stand against the world (Martin, 2016 book). History is rife with examples of individuals who were right while a large part of the world was wrong—Socrates, Hypatia and Galileo, to name a few.

Individuals can be wrong, but corporations are a far darker beast. They, like governments, are groups with the power of many to deprive individuals of their liberty or life. They are designed for one thing: profit.

Now, I happen to like the idea of productivity and earning an honest dollar, deutschmark, or peso. Profit is basically a good thing. But the environment of selfishness borne out of the seed of every corporation is anathema to life on Earth. Why is this so?

While every corporation may start out with a beneficial product or service in mind, the drive for ever-increasing profits creates a blindness in its corporate officers. The corporation will not survive without profits. Their primary focus is on satisfying their investors—the stockholders—and not the customers. Read that last sentence again to let the horrible truth sink in. Customers are *not* the primary focus of corporations. They never are. The focus is *always* on the shareholder. If you go to a stockholder's meeting, I seriously doubt if you will ever hear about customer satisfaction or people cured. The focus is always on profits—units sold and cutting costs.

Though delivering a good product can seem to benefit this notion of profitability, the focus is always on the profits and never on customers or their benefits. The customer is merely a means to an end; a cash cow to be milked until dry. That may seem callous and overly simplistic, but look at what has happened in the health industry. Cures have been out-lawed! And the reason is blindingly obvious.

There are several cures for cancer proven to have been very effective, but each one has been kicked out of the United States. Cures are bad for profits, even though they are wonderful for the patients.

Instead of loving to help customers, corporations love to have continued profits from each customer. The motivation is entirely selfish. If a patient remains alive, but ill, then those patients could generate years of profits for a corporation. See? Simple. So, the incentive for all medical corporations is to prolong the illness while treating the symptoms. Instead of "health maintenance," corporations deal in "disease main-tenance." Let the ghoulishness of this reality penetrate your mind and ego. This is the harsh reality of corporate profits.

Any corporate officer who ever suggests producing cures for a disease will be summarily drummed out of the corporation. After hundreds of billions of dollars spent, and millions of man-hours in research, zero cancer cures have been found by corporations. But plenty of maintenance drugs have been developed.

Corporations have also fast-tracked many of their drugs, using their former employees in government agencies to push them through the government approval process. Profits go up. And if patients die in too great a number, the drug is pulled locally, and sold to third world nations. If corporations are taken to court, they pay millions in fines, but these are small compared to the billions in profits. Corpo-rations may even break the law by killing so many customers, but corporate officers rarely, if ever, go to jail for their mayhem.

Genetically modified organisms (GMOs) is another hot button item. I love the ingenuity of genetic engineering, but the safety protocols for their release into nature are next to nil. When Monsanto produced their first GMO crop, they did 3 months of tests. There were some indications of problems, but they were labeled *statistically insignificant*. The American Food and Drug Administration (FDA), with executives who used to work at Monsanto, approved Monsanto's use and sale of GMO crops. Scientists within the FDA had protested, but the execs overruled their protests.

Later, when French scientist Gilles-Eric Séralini tested the same type of mice for a far longer period, he found that the animals demonstrated severe health problems after 4 months. By 12 months, some of the animals had cancerous tumors a fourth of their body weight. That's huge. On a human, that would be equivalent to a basketball-sized tumor or larger.

Séralini published his findings at Elsevier, a publisher of science journals. Monsanto and their friends protested. A year later, Séralini's paper and one other critical of Monsanto were retracted. The reason for the Séralini retraction was that the paper was "inconclusive." This was a first in science! They invented a new category in order to make Séralini's paper go away. Some months later, independent researchers discovered that the science journal had hired one Richard Goodman as a new editor. Goodman had formerly worked at Monsanto (Corbett). After the retraction, Goodman left the science journal. Thankfully, Séralini was able to find another journal. They doubled the peer review of the article, approved it and republished it, all to the shame of Elsevier and Monsanto.

What does this prove? It shows that corporations don't care about the health of people—their customers. They care far more about profits. They will say anything to appear benign. Why not? If appearing friendly and helpful will increase profits, they'll do all manner of back flips to look good to the masses of customers.

Is there a solution? One might be to boycott *all* corporations. Cut all ties with them. They have become a cancer on the planet—a plague in society. While capitalism is a potentially good idea, in practice it proves itself to be toxically selfish, and incurably so. Like a snake or a scorpion, you cannot train a corporation to change its behavior. So long as the focus is on only profits, it will continue to put profits first, and all other considerations a distant second, or third.

Replace corporations with a different economic paradigm. I suspect that nothing will ever be perfect, so long as there are selfish people in the world. But so long as we have aggressive, confident, altruistic people, we have a chance to make the world a better place. Power is not the problem; selfish attachment to power is the problem.

Like the fight to vindicate carbon dioxide and to restore its abundance, we should also attempt to restore the abundance of human spirit that looks outward, instead of inward—the spirit of the heroic adventurer, instead of the victim—love and generosity, rather than selfishness.

Shell Game

Corporations are owned by people (globalists) who love the money they make, but love power far more. If you think carefully about this, you'll realize that the ultimate in power is ownership and control of the entire planet. This is the ultimate "gold ring" in their game. Mere mortals such as you or I hardly ever think of such things.

The individuals who own the corporations (globalists) are no dummies. They may not be terribly smart, but they understand how some things work. They understand human nature enough to know that it can be manipulated. They know how to get people to wish for things they don't want. They know how to play the marketing shell game to pluck the strings of individual fears and desires.

The environment is one such string. Their marketers surveyed the world and found that people care deeply about the world on which we live. They found others who care more deeply about jobs and families. The globalists have used their think tanks and marketers to sculpt the conflict between these and other opposing groups. On the one side are people who care about the environment and see corporations and their minions as selfish. On the other side are people who don't see themselves as minions so much as realists. They care about balance, but care more about the economy and their prosperity. These are the perfect seeds of division and war.

The globalists continue to fan the flames of division. The Warming Alarmists have "science" on their side and authority of the UN, NASA and many other scientific organizations. Their opposition is funded by big oil, corrupted by religion and conspiracy theories.

The Climate Realists have empirical evidence (science) on their side, and don't need any authority other than the evidence. Their opposition relies on a corrupt corporate news media which promotes "scientific consensus" and "settled science," both of which are oxymorons.

The globalists, through their corporations, control governments, including the United States. Politicians don't get elected unless they have the money to sell their campaigns to the public. And corporations have the money, sometimes funding both sides of a political fight. Lobbyists spend several million dollars per congressman. Anyone who doesn't think this buys influence is living in a world of delusion. There has been a coup and it was won, not with bullets, but with dollars.

But why would we be having governments push to lower carbon dioxide levels if corporations control governments? Doesn't big oil want us to burn more fossil fuels?

Why would we be having biggest oil Rockefellers start the "climate change" movement through their UN front man, the late Maurice Strong (also big oil)? Why would big oil be supporting both sides of the debate? Look further back through history. Why would a major banking family fund both sides of nearly every war since 1800? There may be two key reasons:

1.   Double the profits, and
2.   Control over the outcome.

Several decades ago, during the vetting process in US Congress to approve Nelson Rockefeller as vice president, the man was asked about one of his companies funneling aid to the North Vietnamese. Rockefeller claimed ignorance and the matter was dropped. Here, a matter of treason was mentioned and then ignored. Supporting both sides of the conflict affords greater profits and control over the outcome. When you're a globalist, the nation of your birth is not where your heart is. Nelson's brother, David, later wrote in his *Memoirs,* that he was proud of having conspired for decades against the best interests of the United States.

The Real Reason Behind the Climate Change Hoax

Cooling the planet in an ongoing Ice Age, and lowering CO_2 levels in an era of carbon dioxide starvation, are not idle goals. The Rockefellers and their ilk view the bulk of humanity as "useless eaters"—an unsustainable mass of dead weight on the planet's resources. The Rockefellers are avowed eugenicists. They want to cull the excess population, but it's not easy to murder 7 billion people. Clever marketers have concocted a way for the majority of those "useless eaters" to demand their own deaths. They want to cool the planet, because it will save their nation from being flooded. They want to lower CO_2, because it will save the environment, or so they're told.

The globalists are playing a dangerous game. One simple miscalculation in cooling the planet or lowering the CO_2 levels could result in mass extinctions of life on this world, not to mention the deaths of billions of our fellow humans. Think about it for a moment. If only 50,000 humans could survive at any one time during the last glacial period because of a lack of rain and food, how many of the 7 billion people who currently populate the Earth will survive the start of the next glacial period?

Our technology can help, but the infrastructure of our technological civilization could break apart and quite possibly die. We need to prepare against that possibility. And we need a decentralized effort not based on selfishness.

CO_2 is vital to life. And humans burning fossil fuels have already prolonged the life on this world. But there is much more that needs to be done.

Other books to consider:

'Shining a Light' series

Thermophobia: Shining a Light on Global Warming by Rod Martin, Jr. How the scare is upside-down. How science has become corrupted by big money and fancy marketing, and what we can do to protect our future.

Dirt Ordinary: Shining a Light on Conspiracies by Rod Martin, Jr. These days, the popular notion in America is that conspiracies are fantasies. Other places, not so much. But conspiracies are dirt ordinary with at least 489 new conspiracies starting every second. This book reveals the dangers of conspiracies and what we can do about them.

Favorable Incompetence: Shining a Light on 9/11 by Rod Martin, Jr. How the official conspiracy theory is full of holes, and how that tragedy is becoming increasingly relevant.

Books on Solutions

The Spark of Creativity: How to Unleash a Flood of Ideas That Matter, Right Now by Rod Martin, Jr. Overcoming writer's block and every other possible barrier to your own creativity.

Taking Charge: How to assert positive control over your own emotions by Rod Martin, Jr. It's all about taking charge of your life.

The Art of Forgiveness by Rod Martin, Jr. How 3 miracles on Wilshire Boulevard, Los Angeles led to a number of spiritual breakthroughs in understanding forgiveness and our true spiritual nature. The burden of tragedy can be lifted if you know how. This book gives you the tips you need to achieve the freshness of True Forgiveness.

Discount available on most ebook titles at
http://TharsisHighlands.WordPress.com/books/.

Appendix

- References
- Links to Illustrations
- About Rod Martin, Jr.
- Other Books by Rod Martin, Jr.
- Connect with Rod Martin, Jr.

References

Alley, Richard. (2000). "Holocene Epoch: Subatlantic Chronozone." Retrieved on 2016:0613 from http://s90.photobucket.com/user/dhm1353/media/Climate%20Change/Subatlantic_Had.png.html

Archive.org. (2012:0127). "Temperature -vs- CO2: Last 800,000 Years." Retrieved on 2016:0618 from http://web.archive.org/web/20120127155937/http://robertb.darkhorizons.org/TempGr/Vostok.JPG

Bastasch, Michael. (2015:1217). "EXCLUSIVE: NOAA Relies On 'Compromised' Thermometers That Inflate US Warming Trend." Retrieved on 2016:1104 from http://dailycaller.com/2015/12/17/exclusive-noaa-relies-on-compromised-thermometers-that-inflate-u-s-warming-trend/

BBC. (2009:0210). "HD: Polar Bear on Thin Ice - Nature's Great Events: The Great Melt - BBC One." Retrieved on 2016:1021 from https://youtube.com/watch?v=Kv9v9ALV3yk

Becker, Jo, and Shane, Scott. (2012:0529). "Secret 'Kill List'
        Proves a Test of Obama's Principles and Will."
        Retrieved on 2016:1026 from
        http://nytimes.com/2012/05/29/world/obamas-
        leadership-in-war-on-al-qaeda.html

Booker, Christopher. (2015:0207). "The fiddling with
        temperature data is the biggest science scandal ever."
        Retrieved on 2016:1104 from
        http://telegraph.co.uk/news/earth/environment/globalw
        arming/11395516/The-fiddling-with-temperature-data-
        is-the-biggest-science-scandal-ever.html

Broecker, W.S. (1998). "The End of the Present Interglacial:
        How and When?" Quaternary Science Reviews, Vol. 17,
        pp. 689-694, 1998.

CBC. (ND). "The Ice Storm of 1998." Retrieved on 2016:1026
        from http://cbc.ca/archives/topic/the-ice-storm-of-1998

Cohen, Tamara. (2013:0919). "World's top climate scientists
        told to 'cover up' the fact that the Earth's temperature
        hasn't risen for the last 15 years." Retrieved on
        2016:1104 from http://dailymail.co.uk/news/article-
        2425775/Climate-scientists-told-cover-fact-Earths-
        temperature-risen-15-years.html

Connolly, Ronan, and Connolly, Michael. (2013:1205).
        "Summary: 'Urbanization bias' — Papers 1–3."
        Retrieved on 2016:1104 from
        http://globalwarmingsolved.com/2013/12/summary-
        urbanization-bias-papers-1-3/

Corbett, James. (2013:1203). "Genetic Fallacy: How Monsanto
        Silences Scientific Dissent." Retrieved on 2014:0108
        from https://youtube.com/watch?v=ShJTcIlTna0

CropsReview.com. (ND). "Plant Types: I. C3 Plants,
        Comparison with C4 and CAM Plants." Retrieved on
        2016:1028 from http://cropsreview.com/c3-plants.html

CropsReview.com. (ND). "Plant Types: II. C4 Plants,
    Examples, and C4 Families." Retrieved on 2016:1028
    from http://cropsreview.com/c4-plants.html

CropsReview.com. (ND). "Plant Types: III. CAM Plants,
    Examples and Plant Families." Retrieved on 2016:1028
    from http://cropsreview.com/cam-plants.html

D'Aleo, Joseph. (2009:1013). "How bad is the global
    temperature data?" Retrieved on 2016:1104 from
    https://wattsupwiththat.com/2009/10/13/how-bad-is-
    the-global-temperature-data/

EngineeringToolbox.com. (ND). "Carbon Dioxide
    Concentration - Comfort Levels." Retrieved on
    2016:1026 from http://engineeringtoolbox.com/co2-
    comfort-level-d_1024.html

Fairbanks, R. (1989:1207). "A 17,000-year glacio-eustatic sea
    level record: influence of glacial melting rates on the
    Younger Dryas event and deep-ocean circulation,"
    Nature, Vol. 342.

Georgia State University. (ND). "Systems of Photosynthesis."
    Retrieved on 2016:1026 from http://hyperphysics.phy-
    astr.gsu.edu/hbase/biology/phoc.html

Gerhart, Laci M., and Ward, Joy K. (2010:0705). "Plant
    responses to low [CO2] of the past." Retrieved on
    2016:1027 from
    http://onlinelibrary.wiley.com/doi/10.1111/j.1469-
    8137.2010.03441.x/pdf

Haby, Jeff. (ND). "What Causes the Wind to Blow?" Retrieved
    on 2016:1103 from
    http://theweatherprediction.com/basic_weather_questi
    ons/wind.html

Heller, Tony. (2014:0623). "NOAA/NASA Dramatically
    Altered US Temperatures After The Year 2000."
    Retrieved on 2016:1104 from

https://stevengoddard.wordpress.com/2014/06/23/noaa nasa-dramatically-altered-us-temperatures-after-the-year-2000/

Humlum, Ole. (ND). "10,700 years — GISP2 — with CO2 from EPICA DOME C." Retrieved on 2016:0613 from http://climate4you.com/images/GISP2%20Temperature Since10700%20BP%20with%20CO2%20from%20EPICA%20DomeC.gif

James, John T., Macatangay, Ariel. (ND). "Carbon Dioxide - Our Common 'Enemy'." Retrieved on 2016:1029 from https://ntrs.nasa.gov/archive/nasa/casi.ntrs.nasa.gov/20 090029352.pdf

Kollipara, Puneet. (2014:0122). "Earth Won't Die as Soon as Thought." Retrieved on 2016:1029 from http://sciencemag.org/news/2014/01/earth-wont-die-soon-thought

Lamb, Hubert H. (2012:1124). *Climate: Present, Past and Future: Volume 2: Climatic History and the Future.* Routledge Revivals, Abingdon-on-Thames, UK.

Law, Jennifer, Watkins, Sharmi, *et al.* (2010:06). "In-Flight Carbon Dioxide Exposures and Related Symptoms: Association, Susceptibility, and Operational Implications." Retrieved on 2016:1029 from https://ston.jsc.nasa.gov/collections/trs/_techrep/TP-2010-216126.pdf

LoGiurato, Brett. (2013:0625). "Obama's Climate Joke About A 'Flat Earth Society' Actually Referenced A Real Group." Retrieved on 2016:1025 from http://businessinsider.com/flat-earth-society-to-obama-climate-change-speech-georgetown-2013-6

Lovelock, J.E. & Whitfield, M. (1982:0408) "Lifespan of the Biosphere." *Nature* 296, 561–563.

Manning, Katie, Timpson, Adrian. (2014:0701). "The demographic response to Holocene climate change in the Sahara." Retrieved on 2016:1103 from http://sciencedirect.com/science/article/pii/S0277379114002728

Martin, Rod. (2010:0509). "Atlantis Quest—Uncovering the Secrets that Prove Plato Right." Retrieved on 2010:0509 from http://hubpages.com/education/Atlantis-Quest-Uncovering-the-Secrets-that-Prove-Plato-Right

Martin, Rod. (2016:0719). "Top 10 Climate Change Lies Exposed." Retrieved on 2016:0719 from https://youtube.com/watch?v=ICGal_8qI8c

Martin, Rod. (2016:0826). *Thermophobia: Shining a Light on Global Warming*. Tharsis Highlands, Cebu, Philippines.

Maue, Ryan. (2014:0930). "Global Hurricane Frequency." Retrieved on 2015:1114 from http://policlimate.com/tropical/global_major_freq.png

Maue, Ryan. (2014:0930). "Global Tropical Cyclone Accumulated Cyclone Energy (ACE). Retrieved on 2015:1114 from http://policlimate.com/tropical/global_running_ace.png

McKitrick, Ross. (ND). "The Graph of Temperature vs. Number of Stations." Retrieved on 2016:1104 from http://uoguelph.ca/~rmckitri/research/nvst.html

Mortensen, Lars. (2004). "Doomsday Called Off." Retrieved on 2016:1107 from https://youtube.com/watch?v=Pg_2fJImqac [http://www.imdb.com/title/tt0493121/]

Mortensen, Lars. (2008). "The Cloud Mystery." Retrieved on 2015:1015 from https://youtube.com/watch?v=ANMTPF1blpQ [http://imdb.com/title/tt2005265/]

NASA. (2013:0203). "Consensus: 97% of climate scientists agree." Retrieved on 2015:0728 from http://climate.nasa.gov/scientific-consensus/

NOAA. (ND). "GISP2 Volcanic Markers." Retrieved on 2008:0801 from ftp://ftp.ncdc.noaa.gov/pub/data/paleo/icecore/greenland/summit/gisp2/chem/volcano.txt

Norris, Richard. (ND). "Cretaceous Thermal Maximum ~85-90 Ma." Retrieved on 2016:1103 from http://scrippsscholars.ucsd.edu/rnorris/book/cretaceous-thermal-maximum-85-90-ma

Painting, Rob. (ND). "Positives and negatives of global warming: Intermediate" Retrieved 2016:0611 from http://skepticalscience.com/argument.php?f=global-warming-positives-negatives&l=2

Phys.org. (2012:0614). "Warm climate -- cold Arctic? The Eemian is a poor analogue for current climate change." Retrieved on 2016:1026 from http://phys.org/news/2012-06-climate-cold-arctic-eemian.html

Retro Report. (2015:0616). "Taking the Lid Off the McDonald's Coffee Case." Retrieved on 2017:0130 from https://retroreport.org/video/taking-the-lid-off-the-mcdonalds-coffee-case/

Rose, David. (2015:0119). "Nasa climate scientists: We said 2014 was the warmest year on record... but we're only 38% sure we were right." Retrieved on 2016:0119 from http://dailymail.co.uk/news/article-2915061/Nasa-climate-scientists-said-2014-warmest-year-record-38-sure-right.html

Sage, Rowan F., and Zhu, Xin-Guang. (2011). "Exploiting the engine of C4 photosynthesis." Retrieved on 2016:1029

from
http://jxb.oxfordjournals.org/content/62/9/2989.full.pdf

SciJinks. (2016:1018). "Why does wind blow?" Retrieved on
2016:1103 from http://scijinks.jpl.nasa.gov/wind/

Spencer, Dr. Roy. (ND). "Latest Global Temps." Retrieved on
2016:1104 from http://drroyspencer.com/latest-global-
temperatures/

Swann, Ben. (2012:0904). "Reality Check: 1 on 1 With
President Obama, How Does He Justify A Kill List?"
Retrieved on 2012:0905 from
https://youtube.com/watch?v=WrRuNOaNYME

University of Copenhagen. (ND). "A glimpse into the
Eemian." Retrieved on 2015:0807 from
http://iceandclimate.nbi.ku.dk/research/climatechange/
glacial_interglacial/eemian/

Watts, Anthony. (ND). "Weather Stations." Retrieved on
2016:1104 from
https://wattsupwiththat.com/category/weather_stations
/

Watts, Anthony. (2012:0730). "Surface Stations, A resource for
climate station records and surveys." Retrieved on
2016:1104 from http://surfacestations.org/

Watts, Anthony. (2013:1014). "90 climate model projectons
versus reality." Retrieved on 2016:1102 from
https://wattsupwiththat.com/2013/10/14/90-climate-
model-projectons-versus-reality/

Watts, Anthony. (2014:0328). "IPCC admission from new
report: 'no evidence climate change has led to even a
single species becoming extinct'." Retrieved on
2016:1102 from
https://wattsupwiththat.com/2014/03/28/ipcc-
admission-from-new-report-no-evidence-climate-

change-has-led-to-even-a-single-species-becoming-extinct/

Watts, Anthony. (2015:0403). "Claim: polar bears can't subsist on anything but seals." Retrieved on 2016:1028 from https://wattsupwiththat.com/2015/04/03/claim-polar-bears-cant-subsist-on-anything-but-seals/

WeatherWizKids.com. (ND). "Wind." Retrieved on 2016:1103 from http://weatherwizkids.com/weather-wind.htm

Wikipedia.org. (ND). "January 1998 North American ice storm." Retrieved on 2016:1026 from https://en.wikipedia.org/wiki/January_1998_North_American_ice_storm

Glossary

Note: Not every term or concept has been included in this glossary. I encourage you to explore the subject online or in books on those terms for which you would like more information. Make learning a lifetime occupation.

carbon dioxide *n.* —an odorless, colorless gas and a minor constituent of the Earth's atmosphere. Without this trace gas, all life on Earth would die. Frequently abbreviated CO_2. This is what plants breathe. And plants "exhale" oxygen (which see). Not to be confused with poisonous carbon monoxide (CO).

climate *n.* —a persistent average state of a region's weather, typically taken over a period of several decades— usually thirty years.

climate change *n.* —modification of a region's persisting average weather. This can include warming or cooling, alterations in turbulence, patterns of flow, timing of events, atmospheric chemistry and more. Such modifications have occurred throughout the existence of our planet's atmosphere—more than 4 billion years. This term has been kidnapped by a modern movement to mean only "recent, manmade, warming and catastrophic" modifications to the atmosphere. This is a distortion of the original definition.

CO_2 *n.*—carbon dioxide (which see).

drought *n.*—a period of decreased rainfall that is insufficient for the life forms within a region. Drought typically occurs from changes in weather patterns, but more importantly from regional or global cooling. In fact, the global cooling of the last 50 million years or so has significantly desiccated the planet, increasing the extent of subtropical deserts and creating polar deserts.

Earth *n.*—our home planet. It possesses a breathable atmosphere, water in three key phases (solid, liquid, gas), dry land and a surface teeming with life. It also has one natural satellite typically called the Moon.

glacial *n.*—a cooler period of increased glaciation during an Ice Age in which polar glaciers expand to cover large portions of adjacent continents. During the last 1.1 million years of the current Ice Age, glacial periods have averaged 90,000 years in length (ref: W.S. Broecker, 1998). The duration of glacial periods for the last 800,000 years has varied between 24,000 and 143,000 years. Compare *interglacial*.

global cooling *n.*—a decrease in the average temperature of the planet. This can be a bad thing during our current Ice Age. Cooling tends to produce less evaporation, and thus drier climate.

global warming *n.*—an increase in the average temperature of the planet. This can be a good thing during our current Ice Age. Warming tends to produce more evaporation, and thus moister climate.

Holocene *n.*—an interglacial of the current Ice Age; the current interglacial (which see).

Holocene Optimum *n.*—a period of about 3,000 years wherein the northern hemisphere was as much as 1.1°C warmer than today. This warmth, compared with the shallow cool periods (roughly as warm as today) resulted in a green Sahara for about 3,000 years.

hurricane *n.*—A dangerous tropical cyclone of the Atlantic Ocean region. Compare *typhoon*.

Ice Age *n.*—a period of increased cooling where both polar regions experience permanent glaciation throughout the year. The current such period has had glaciation in Greenland and Antarctica for roughly 2.6 million years. Such periods include several glacial and interglacial periods, alternating between warmer and cooler phases.

interglacial *n.*—a warmer period of relaxed glaciation during an Ice Age in which polar glaciation recedes and global climate warms noticeably. The amount of warming and glacial receding can vary a great deal with some such periods being as much as 5°C warmer than our current Modern Warm Period, or 2°C cooler. There have been several dozen interglacials in the current Ice Age. For the last 1.1 million years, interglacials have averaged about 11,000 years in length (ref: W.S. Broecker, 1998). The duration of interglacial periods for the last 800,000 years has varied between 4,000 and 24,000 years. Compare *glacial*.

Intergovernmental Panel on Climate Change *n.*—a political organization associated with the United Nations tasked with determining the nature and extent of man's impact on the planetary climate as a result of burning fossil fuels.

IPCC *n.*—Intergovernmental Panel on Climate Change (which see).

Jupiter *n.*—the largest planet in our star system, roughly ten times the diameter of Earth, with a thick atmosphere many thousands of kilometers deep and no solid surface. Because of its great distance from the sun, it is extremely cold at the tops of the clouds, near the air pressure equivalent to that on Earth's surface. Despite the extreme cold, the planet hosts some of the largest storms in the solar system.

oxygen *n.*—a key constituent of Earth's atmosphere and the most vital gas for animal life. Animals exhale carbon dioxide (which see).

parts per million *n.*—the concentration of something as a fractional measure compared to a whole. If you take a million of something, the count given will be the number of pieces or portions out of that whole million that apply to a specific substance. This is similar to the term percent. Example: The atmosphere consists of 21 percent oxygen, or 210,000 parts per million oxygen.

Pleistocene *n.*—the current Ice Age (which see). This period of permanent polar glaciation has lasted for 2.6 million years. Before scientists knew very much about Earth's history, they thought the Pleistocene ended 11,600 years ago. Today, we know that the current epoch—the Holocene—is merely one in a series of dozens of interglacial periods that are part of this Ice Age.

ppm *abbr.*—parts per million (which see).

tornado *n.*—a small, cyclonic storm, typically less than several hundred meters across, with extremely fast winds and an ability to create tremendous damage to buildings and to anything else above ground.

typhoon *n.*—a dangerous tropical cyclone of the Pacific Ocean region. Compare *hurricane*.

Venus *n.*—our sister planet, closer to the sun. The planet is slightly smaller than Earth (which see), has a crushing atmosphere of mostly CO_2, a heavily reflective cloud cover, and a surface with virtually no wind and temperatures hot enough to melt lead (462°C). The planet spins very, very slowly and has no natural satellite.

warm period *n.*—a span of time which has a higher temperature than the preceding and succeeding spans of time. Climate always changes and most frequently in repeating cycles. The Holocene has contained 10 clearly-defined major warm periods on a roughly 1,000-year cycle. Cycles of other periods make the pattern of warming and cooling more complex than they would be if there were only one cycle involved. The most recent four major warm periods of the Holocene have been, the Modern (1850 to today), the Medieval (850–1350), the Roman (200 BC–AD 100) and the Minoan (1400–1100 BC).

Links to Illustrations

Chapter 1 — 15,000 BC, Dodging the CO_2 Extinction Bullet

Barnola, Jean-Marc, *et al*. (ND). "Vostok, Antarctica, Ice-core CO2 Record." Retrieved on 2016:1016 from http://cdiac.ornl.gov/trends/co2/graphics/vostok.co2.gif

Chapter 2 — CO_2 Starvation

Illis, Bill. (2014:0614). "CO2 Last 40 Million Years." Retrieved on 2016:1016 from https://wattsupwiththat.com/reference-pages/atmosphere-page/co2-page/

Videography

Be sure to Like, Comment and Subscribe to the channel:
https://youtube.com/c/RodMartinJr/

Climate Change Lies Exposed series

Top 10 Climate Change Lies Exposed
https://youtube.com/watch?v=ICGal_8qI8c
Climate Change Lie #1 Exposed: Global Warming is Bad
https://youtube.com/watch?v=KbfjEPo083U
Climate Change Lie #2 Exposed: CO2 Causes Dangerous
Global Warming
https://youtube.com/watch?v=ZH5ATcpMJQo
Climate Change Lie #3 Exposed: Global Warming Causes
Extreme Weather
https://youtube.com/watch?v=aTiBbAGl0qI
Climate Change Lie #4 Exposed: Global Warming causes
droughts
https://youtube.com/watch?v=DusZ5dP4hDw
Climate Change Lie #5 Exposed: Our current warmth is
unusual
https://youtube.com/watch?v=FR2aZc5bjUU

Climate Change Lie #6 Exposed: Our current level of CO2 is
unusually high
https://youtube.com/watch?v=ASV3UUwYZg0
Climate Change Lie #7 Exposed: The rate of warming is
dangerous
https://youtube.com/watch?v=OsJ67Hp4l-g
Climate Change Lie #8 Exposed: The Science is Settled
https://youtube.com/watch?v=6yzkAjWY8rM
Climate Change Lie #9 Exposed — There is a consensus on
dangerous, man made, Global Warming
https://youtube.com/watch?v=URE4NMk1DbA

Carbon Dioxide Fan Club

Earth vs. Venus: Will our world ever suffer runaway
greenhouse warming?
https://youtube.com/watch?v=SO1M8GEDyYk
Top 10 Facts that Prove CO2 Does NOT Drive Global
Temperature
https://youtube.com/watch?v=CSQlJx76b64
Verdict: CO2 Not Guilty! Greenhouse DESTROYED! Must see!
https://youtube.com/watch?v=1f6zB320Hac

Global Warming Fan Club

How Global Warming Made Civilization Possible
https://youtube.com/watch?v=057GgxpZWRc
Top 10 Reasons Global Warming is Good
https://youtube.com/watch?v=dQc4iXgrrEo

Big Climate Quiz (BCQ)

BCQ #1: Why didn't civilization start during the last glacial
period?
https://youtube.com/watch?v=Bf0gty2XAjw
BCQ #2: What Causes Wind to Blow?

https://youtube.com/watch?v=lhk7JIQ6e-U
BCQ #3: How does land ever get water?
https://youtube.com/watch?v=do0kb7Udq-g
BCQ #4: What is an Ice Age?
https://youtube.com/watch?v=RjMbE-G8JFo

Climate Music Video series

Thermophobia - Why Fear of Warming in the current Ice Age is all wrong
https://youtube.com/watch?v=Q68fIkdC9Rk
Extreme Weather - How the Climate Change Alarm is All Wrong
https://youtube.com/watch?v=x18gwLpLI2A
Thermophobia -- Debunking: "Global Warming causes more storms"
https://youtube.com/watch?v=d40_2yGuV_o

About Rod Martin, Jr.

Rod Martin, Jr. is a modern polymath (Renaissance man)— artist, scientist, mathematician, engineer and philosopher. He first became interested in climate science in the mid-70s. A forest ecology PhD friend of his was retiring and donated two climate texts to the cause. Initially, his interest in the subject covered planetary atmospheres—weather systems, atmospheric retention rates, optical thickness (greenhouse effect), adiabatic lapse rates, climate chemistry and planetary habitability.

Like so many others, during the 70s, 80s and 90s, Martin's interest in ecology and the environment continued to grow. When Al Gore's film, *An Inconvenient Truth*, came out in 2006, Martin was an immediate fan. But as the controversy on the topic heated up, Martin suddenly realized that all of the things he had learned about climate over the years contradicted many of the so-called facts in Gore's award-winning film.

In college, from the mid-90s to the early 2000s, Martin studied computer science, earning a degree, *summa cum laude*.

With only a 139 IQ, Martin realized that he was not the sharpest implement in the tool shed. In fact, all of his younger brothers had far higher IQs. From this relative handicap, he learned the immense value of humility and the need to remain unattached to any ideas, lest they become dogma, and blind him from further discovery. Thus, he was able to learn the true value of skepticism, and was able to recognize the inevitable pitfalls of that scientific paradigm. He also made the distinction between confidence in knowledge (an enormous source of blindness) and confidence in one's ability to find new knowledge (a source of empowerment).

In 2016, Martin implemented a campaign to set the record straight on climate. He wasn't alone. Many climate scientists, astrophysicists, meteorologists and concerned citizens had already begun to speak out against the so-called "scientific consensus" (an oxymoron, because science is never done by consensus). Martin has created numerous educational videos on climate change and global warming and created a website to discuss these topics in greater detail.

https://GlobalWarmthBlog.WordPress.com/

From a lasting love of stars and astronomy, he created 3D space software, "Stars in the NeighborHood," available online.

https://SpaceSoftware.WordPress.com/buy-now/

He currently resides in the Philippines with his wife, Juvy.

He has taught mathematics, information technology, critical thinking and professional ethics at Benedicto College, Mandaue City, Cebu. He continues to teach online and to write.

Other Books by Rod Martin, Jr.

Non-Fiction (as Rod Martin, Jr.)

The Art of Forgiveness, Tharsis Highlands (2012, 2015)

The Bible's Hidden Wisdom: God's Reason for Noah's Flood, Tharsis Highlands (2014)

The Spark of Creativity, Tharsis Highlands (2014)

Dirt Ordinary: Shining a Light on Conspiracies, Tharsis Highlands (2015)

Favorable Incompetence: Shining a Light on 9/11, Tharsis Highlands (2015)

Thermophobia: Shining a Light on Global Warming, Tharsis Highlands (2016)

Red Line—Carbon Dioxide: How humans saved all life on Earth by burning fossil fuels, Tharsis Highlands (2016)

The Science of Miracles: How Scientific Method Can Be Applied to Spiritual Phenomena, Tharsis Highlands (2018)

Proof of God, Tharsis Highlands (2018)

Deserts & Droughts: How does Land Ever Get Water?, Tharsis Highlands (2018)

Taking Charge: How to Assert Positive Control Over Your Own Emotions, Tharsis Highlands (2018)

Spirit is Digital — Science is Analog: Discovering where miracles and logic intersect, Tharsis Highlands (2019)
Proof of Atlantis? Evidence of Plato's Lost Island Empire, Tharsis Highlands (2019)
Enemies of Christ: The Need to Protect Our Own Salvation from Ravening Wolves, Tharsis Highlands (2019)

Science Fiction (as Carl Martin)

Touch the Stars: Emergence, with John Dalmas, Tor (1983), *expanded* Tharsis Highlands (2012)
Touch the Stars: Diaspora, Book 2 of Touch the Stars, Tharsis Highlands (2014)
Entropy's Children, anthology of short fiction, Tharsis Highlands (2014)
Gods and Dragons, Book 1 of *Edge of Remembrance,* Tharsis Highlands (2017)
Tales of Atlantis Lost, Book 2 of *Edge of Remembrance,* Tharsis Highlands (2017)

An Excerpt from *Thermophobia*

Introduction: Thermophobia in Perspective

"One of the brightest gems in the New England weather is the dazzling uncertainty of it." — Mark Twain, speech to the New England Society, December 22, 1876

Thermophobia is a fear of warmth — a disease which has gripped much of the planet in recent years. Every fear about global warming will be cured in this book. We will use facts, logic, science and a sense of perspective that has been sorely missing from much of the mainstream media. Don't misunderstand this. Caring about the planet and our future is the foundation of this book.

Let us start with some simple questions.

Do you fear cuddling? Do you shake in terror over the idea of wrapping up in a warm blanket on a cold, rainy or snowy night? Does the notion of a warm bath or shower send chills up your spine? And do you stand frozen in horror thinking about sitting down to a nice, hot meal?

No?

Then why has civilization gone suddenly bonkers over a rise in average global temperature of 5.4 °F (3 °C) *over the next century?* That's a temperature difference some people would be hard pressed to discern. That's a yearly increase of only 0.06 °F (0.035 °C), barely enough to be measurable by most and felt by none. When a similar, natural rate of warming delivered us from the frozen horrors of the Little Ice Age, no one complained.

Let's do some comparison.

Downtown Los Angeles has a coastal, Mediterranean-type climate with an average daily high in the rainy month of February of 68.6 °F (20.3 °C) and an average daily low of 49.3 °F (9.6 °C). This gives us a daily range of about 19.3 °F (10.7 °C). *Frightening!* That's more than three times the dreaded increase foretold by the United Nations. But the people in Southern California don't seem to mind. And that's once a day, every day in February. And that's a minor fluctuation, dampened by the weather and proximity to the Pacific Ocean.

Phoenix, Arizona has an inland, high desert climate with an average daily high in dry June of 103.9 °F (39.9 °C) and an average daily low of 77.7 °F (25.4 °C). This gives us a daily range of a whopping 26.2 °F (14.5 °C). *Terrifying!* And yet Phoenix has been such a magnet, its population has grown from nearly 107,000 in 1950 to over 1.4 million in 2010—an increase of nearly 14 times. When my younger brother, Terry, worked for the US Postal Service, he told me they were opening up a new route or two every month just to keep up.

Over a twelve-month period, every year, temperatures in Los Angeles vary from an average low of 47.5 °F (8.6 °C) to an average high of 84.4 °F (29.1 °C). That's a *mind-numbing* yearly change of 36.9 °F (20.5 °C)—nearly seven times the UN's horror story.

For the yearly changes in Phoenix, we might just *blow a gasket.* Temperatures there vary from an average low of 44.8 °F (7.1 °C) to an average high of 106.1 °F (41.2 °C). That's a yearly change of 61.3 °F (34.1 °C)—every year, over eleven times the "global warming" scare story. People in Phoenix are not freaking out over this amount of yearly temperature change. Maybe they know something the UN doesn't.

Climate is a complex, non-linear system which is globally stable and locally unpredictable. This means that the entire planet will experience changes gradually. Simple inputs, however do not necessarily have simple outputs. Increase the water vapor worldwide, and you will tend to increase the potential rainfall overall, but the rainfall at any one location will remain unpredictable. But even that effect is not simple. Global warming will cause more evaporation from the oceans, but it will also result in the air being able to hold more water vapor before it precipitates as rain or snow. Non-linear simply means that the effects are displayed as curves on graphs rather than straight lines. Some of those curves can be quite complex.

Also, there are many things we do not yet know about the processes and effects within the climate and weather systems. We don't yet know the sensitivity of temperature change with changes in carbon dioxide. The paleoclimatic record tends to show that temperature has a relatively low sensitivity to changes in CO_2, but that's only a qualitative assessment. We don't yet know the exact quantity of this sensitivity. Thus, UN climate models will continue to yield outputs which do not match reality. Also, we do not yet know all of the factors which change climate. For instance, we're still studying the processes by which clouds are formed and their effect on overall climate.

More questions!

Where do most people want to vacation—snow or beach—cold climate or warm? Where do New Yorkers like to retire, if they have the money—Greenland or Florida? Which provides a more hospitable environment for growing crops— cold or warm? Where are we more likely to grow the food to feed millions—Antarctica or Java?

If you've been paying attention to the world around you, likely you will give the warmer answer for each of these questions. This seems to be almost a no-brainer, yet the news and government reports are awash with the horrors of global warming! Thus the ironic term, *thermophobia*—a fear of warmth.

In 2013, according to Mike Schneider of *Business Insider*, an estimated 537,000 residents moved to Florida and 10% of them were from New York state—or about 54,000. An estimated zero residents moved to Greenland. Certainly, real estate is far cheaper in Greenland, but facilities and infrastructure are largely nonexistent there. The infrastructure is missing, because the demand is near nonexistent. Warmer climates trump colder ones by a vast margin.

When we compare the population density of various latitudes, we see a clear correlation. Southern United States, including California, Oklahoma, Tennessee, North Carolina and states farther south, have an average density of 49.02 people per square kilometer. Northern states have an average population density of 28.48 people per square kilometer. Southern Canada has 6.82 people per square kilometer, while

Northern Canada drops to 0.16 people per square kilometer. The gradation is clear. People like it warmer.

Below is a map showing the population gradient for the entire world by 10° latitude bands. This is based not on total population, but population per square kilometer of land for each band. Part of the reason for the bias toward the northern hemisphere has to do with the warming effect of the Gulf Stream. That flow of warmer water makes higher latitudes more livable in Europe than they would otherwise be.

In Canada, for instance, the southern border of Northwest Territories stands at 60°N. The closest large city to this latitude is Yellowknife with a population of about 19,000 people. Near that same latitude in Sweden is the capital city, Stockholm. Its metropolitan area has a population of over 2.1 million people. Oslo, Norway has about the same latitude and a metro area population of over 1.7 million.

The amount of warming being predicted as "catastrophic," most people would barely notice. The charts being bandied about by politicians and computer climate modelers show mountains of temperature increase that really are only fractions of a single degree. We're looking at mountains that are visible only under a microscope. The error bars of data sometimes are nearly as large as the swings in the data. In other words, someone is making a big deal out of practically nothing.

https://tharsishighlands.wordpress.com/books/thermophobia-global-warming/

Connect with Rod Martin, Jr.

Rod Martin, Jr. is his pen name for non-fiction. Carl Martin is
      his pen name for fiction.

BitChute—https://bitchute.com/channel/M63WrjRpNSPT/

Minds—https://minds.com/RodMartinJr

Gab—https://gab.ai/RodMartinJr

Website and Blog—https://rodmartinjr.wordpress.com/

HubPages—https://hubpages.com/@lone77star

Smashwords author page—
      https://smashwords.com/profile/view/CarlMartin77

Smashwords author page—
      https://smashwords.com/profile/view/RodMartinJr

Udemy courses page—https://udemy.com/user/rodmartinjr/

Facebook—https://facebook.com/RodMartinJr/

Twitter—https://twitter.com/LoneStar77/

Google+—https://plus.google.com/+RodMartinJr/

YouTube—https://youtube.com/c/RodMartinJr/

Goodreads author page—https://goodreads.com/Carl_Martin

Goodreads author page—
      https://goodreads.com/Rod_Martin_Jr

Amazon author page—https://amazon.com/Carl-
  Martin/e/B008CX8KN6/
Amazon author page—https://amazon.com/Rod-Martin-
  Jr/e/B008CZ9JTS/

www.ingramcontent.com/pod-product-compliance
Lightning Source LLC
Chambersburg PA
CBHW070433290526
45791CB00005B/1962